Gritty
and
Graceful

15 Inspiring Women of the Bible

By Caryn Rivadeneira

Illustrated by Sonya Abby Soekarno

beaming books
MINNEAPOLIS

25 24 23 22 21 20 19   1 2 3 4 5 6 7 8

Hardcover ISBN: 978-1-5064-5206-7

Library of Congress Cataloging-in-Publication Data
Library of Congress Control Number: 2018965131

Beaming Books
510 Marquette Avenue
Minneapolis, MN 55402
Beamingbooks.com

In Memory of Barb Brouwer
Who did great things for God

It wasn't easy to be a girl in Bible times. Girls lived hard lives. People didn't listen to girls. People didn't believe girls. Most of the time, people didn't even *want* girls.

But God wasn't like that. God used girls (and boys!) to do great things. And God did great things for girls!

God made girls good. That's what the Bible says. But the Bible also *shows us* that God made girls with *grit and grace*. That means God made girls strong and kind. God made girls to be gritty and graceful in everything we do. Just like the women of the Bible.

I Am Eve

My husband Adam and I lived in a perfect, sunshiny garden. Until one day, I disobeyed God. God had told us, "Don't eat that fruit. If you do, you will die." But a snake said God was lying. I believed the snake and decided to eat the fruit. So did Adam. Our perfect garden grew dark. We were scared, so we hid from God.

But God found us. When God asked why we disobeyed, Adam blamed me. But God didn't. Instead of blame, God gave me a promise: one day, one of my descendants would save the world from our sin.

God did great things for me—and I did great things for God.

VERSE: "The man named his wife Eve, because she would become the mother of all living."

—Genesis 3:20

I Am Hagar

"Sarah and Abraham, you will have a baby!" That's what God told Sarah. She just laughed. Sarah and Abraham were way too old! So Sarah told me to go to Abraham and give them a baby. I was Sarah's slave and did what she told me to do. I named my baby Ishmael. But Sarah didn't like him. Or me. She sent us to the desert, where we almost died! But God saw me and heard my prayers. God saved us both by sending us water and helping us survive.

God remembered Sarah too, and gave her a baby after many years of waiting. She named her baby Isaac. Even though our circumstances made us enemies, God blessed us both, and made us mothers of great nations.

God did great things for Sarah and me—and we did great things for God.

VERSE: She gave this name to the LORD who spoke to her: "You are the God who sees me."

—Genesis 16:13

I Am Miriam

Pharaoh, the King of Egypt where we lived, wanted to kill all Hebrew babies. *We* were Hebrew. So my mom and I floated my baby brother Moses down the river, praying God would protect him. When Pharaoh's daughter found Moses, my stomach dropped. But then the princess picked him up and cradled him. I told the princess my mom could be Moses' nanny. The princess agreed! Because of what I did, Moses grew up to free our people from slavery. I led alongside him and wrote songs of praise.

God did great things for me—and I did great things for God.

VERSE: Then [Miriam] asked Pharaoh's daughter, "Shall I go and get one of the Hebrew women to nurse the baby for you?" "Yes, go," she answered.

—Exodus 2:7-8

I Am Rahab

Lots of strange men came to my inn—but not many *Hebrew* men did. After all, my city was in Canaan, and we were their enemies. Still, when two Hebrew spies knocked on my door and asked me to hide them, I did what they asked and hid them up on the roof. I had heard about how powerful the Hebrews' God was, and I wanted to know even more.

The king wanted to kill the spies, but I helped them escape through the window. Later, when the Hebrew army attacked my city and the walls came tumbling down, God saved me and my family—and I became part of God's people.

God did great things for me—and I did great things for God.

VERSE: "Now then, please swear to me by the Lord that you will show kindness to my family, because I have shown kindness to you."

—Joshua 2:12

I Am Deborah

I was a prophet, a judge, a poet—
and a warrior. One day, enemies
threatened God's people. Our top
soldier Barak was too afraid to
fight them. But I wasn't afraid—I
was ready. I led 10,000 soldiers
into battle that day. I told the
soldiers that a woman would win
this battle and that God would
deliver us. And because of my
bravery and God's help, that's
exactly what happened.

God did great things for me—and I
did great things for God.

*VERSE: "Certainly I will go with
you," said Deborah. "But because
of the course you are taking,
the honor will not be yours, for
the LORD will deliver Sisera into the
hands of a woman."*

—Judges 4:9

I Am Hannah

I prayed and prayed and prayed for a baby. I promised that if God gave me a baby, I would raise that child to work for God. God answered my prayers, and I kept my promise. When my son Samuel was still little, I took him to the temple to live with the priest. My heart broke when I left my boy behind, but I visited Samuel whenever I could and prayed for him every day. Samuel grew up to be a great man of God. He anointed Israel's first king!

I did great things for God—and God did great things for me.

VERSE: So in the course of time Hannah became pregnant and gave birth to a son. She named him Samuel, saying, "Because I asked the Lord for him."

—1 Samuel 1:20

We Are Naomi and Ruth

I am Naomi. When my husband and sons died, I was sad and angry. But my daughter-in-law Ruth stayed by my side and helped me remember that even though we had lost so much, we still had each other—and God.

I am Ruth. After my husband died, I left everything I knew to move away with Naomi. There, I found a new husband, and God gave us back the home and family Naomi and I had lost.

God saved us and our family—a family that would one day include kings and even the King of Kings!

God did great things for us—and we did great things for God.

VERSE: But Ruth replied, ". . . Where you go I will go, and where you stay I will stay. Your people will be my people and your God my God."

—Ruth 1:16

I Am Queen Esther

The king chose me to be queen because I was beautiful. He didn't know I was also smart—and Jewish. The king's friend Haman hated Jewish people and convinced the king to kill us all. But my uncle told me that this was exactly why God had put me in the palace: to save us all! And he was right. I told the king if he killed all Jewish people, he'd have to kill me. I was scared, but God made me brave. The king punished Haman, and my people were saved!

God did great things for me—and I did great things for God.

VERSE: "Go, gather together all the Jews . . . and fast for me . . . When this is done, I will go to the king, even though it is against the law. And if I perish, I perish."

—Esther 4:16

I Am Mary

One day an angel visited me. I was terrified. The angel said, "Don't be afraid. You make God happy!" The angel told me that God had chosen me to be the mother of the Messiah. But because I wasn't married to Joseph yet, I was confused. How would I have a baby?

Even though I was scared and confused, I said yes to the angel. I said yes to God. Nine months later, Joseph and I traveled to Bethlehem where Jesus—my sweet son and the Savior of the world—was born.

God did great things for me—and I did great things for God.

VERSE: "My soul glorifies the Lord . . . From now on all generations will call me blessed, for the Mighty One has done great things for me."

—Luke 1: 46-49

We Are Mary and Martha

We are sisters. We love each other. And we both followed Jesus. But in every other way, we are as different as can be. Mary loved to listen to Jesus' teachings and poured expensive perfume on his feet. Martha kept busy in the kitchen, making sure everyone was fed and parties ran smoothly. People shamed us both for our choices. Sometimes we even shamed each other. But Jesus loved us both, and we each served Jesus in our own way.

God did great things for us—and we did great things for God.

VERSE: As Jesus and his disciples were on their way, he came to a village where a woman named Martha opened her home to him. She had a sister called Mary, who sat at the Lord's feet listening to what he said.

—Luke 10:38-39

I Am the Woman at the Well

One day, I met a man named Jesus at the water well. It was hot, and Jesus was thirsty. I shared my water with him. Normally, a Jewish man like Jesus wouldn't take anything from a Samaritan woman like me. But Jesus was different. He listened to me and answered my questions. He didn't shame me. He offered me living water. He made me feel loved and forgiven. And Jesus told me—before he told anyone else—that he was the Messiah!

After that, I just had to tell everyone about Jesus. I preached everywhere: *The Messiah has come!*

God did great things for me—and I did great things for God.

VERSE: "When the Messiah comes, he will explain everything to us."

Then Jesus declared, "I am he, the one speaking to you."

—John 4:25-26

The Bleeding Woman

I bled for twelve years. Straight. I couldn't leave the house to shop or be with friends. I was so lonely, because everyone thought I was unclean. Then one day Jesus came to my town. I knew Jesus could heal me if I got near him. So I snuck through the crowds, careful not to touch anyone—except Jesus. I reached out to touch his robe. My bleeding stopped! I was healed!

Then Jesus turned around and asked who touched him. I was terrified as I stepped forward and confessed that I had touched his robe. But Jesus just smiled. He said my faith had healed me!

God did great things for me—and I did great things for God.

VERSE: "If I just touch his clothes, I will be healed."

—Mark 5:27

Mary Magdalene

I met Jesus the day he healed me. After that, I followed Jesus everywhere. I followed Jesus to the cross. I followed Jesus to the tomb. The Sunday morning after his death, I went back to that tomb. But Jesus was gone! I asked a gardener where Jesus was.

Then I heard my name: *Mary*. This wasn't a gardener! This was Jesus! My friend was alive! I hugged Jesus and never wanted to let go. But Jesus told me to go, to tell the disciples the Good News. I was the first follower of Jesus to say: "He is risen!"

God did great things for me—and I did great things for God.

VERSE: Jesus said to her, "Mary." She turned toward him and cried out, "Teacher."

—John 20:16

Caryn Rivadeneira is the author of eleven books for both children and grown-ups. Caryn is a proud member of INK: A Creative Collective and the Society of Children's Book Writers and Illustrators. When not writing, you can find Caryn at her church, where she serves on staff, or hanging out with her husband, three kids, and rescued pit bull.

Sonya Abby Soekarno is an illustrator and visual development artist currently based in San Francisco. Originally from Jakarta, Indonesia, she recently graduated from the Academy of Art University. Sonya's interest for children's book illustrations stem from her love of bright and vibrant colors, as well as the various whimsical fantasies she grew up reading.